REFLECTIONS ON FAITH INSPIRED BY SENIORS

Phil Ridden

EDWEST PUBLISHING

Copyright © Phil Ridden, 2020

Published 2020 by Edwest Publishing
Joondalup, Western Australia
www.edwestpublishing.biz

ISBN: Paperback 978-0-9925481-4-8

The author asserts his moral rights.
No part of this publication may be reproduced or transmitted, in any form or by any means without the permission of the author, except for fair use in worship and study.

To contact the author:
Phil@philridden.biz
www.philridden.biz

CONTENTS

Why this book? vii
Why seniors? viii
A word about Biblical quotes ix
SENIORS THROUGH THEIR OWN EYES 1
DIGNITY 2
BIRTHDAYS 4
YOU CAN'T DIE 6
HEAVEN 8
DOTAGE 10
PILLOW 12
BALD 13
CHANGING VALUES 14
HALO 16
SENSES 18
APPEARANCE 20
LOST GRANDCHILDREN 22
CHECK UP 24
ELDERLY 26
US AND ME 28
FUNERALS 30
OCCASIONAL VISITS 32
LEGACY 33

Phil Ridden *Reflections on faith inspired by seniors*

SENIORS THROUGH YOUNGER EYES 34
JOY 35
SONGS 36
SITTING 37
DRIVING 39
BLIND 41
YELLING 43
COMPLAINING 45
NAPPIES 47
FRIENDSHIP 49
GRIEF 51
HOSPITAL 52
TELEVISION 53
GENERATION 55
GOODBYE 57
DAILY PHONE CALL 58
PLAYFUL 59
SLIPPING AWAY 61
SINGING 63
WISDOM 65
FAÇADE 67
NOT THERE YET 69
WALKING FRAME 71
BLOCKED EARS 72

STRUGGLING	73
GIVING BACK	75
ANGER	77
NEW HIPS	79
RESILIENCE	80
LOVE LETTERS	81
JEWELLERY	83
AGEING	85
DECAY	87
ZIP	88
THE FACE	89
CUTTING UP FOOD	91
INSIGHT	93
LIKE HIM	95
GIVING UP	97
GREAT GRANDPARENTS	99
ALIKE	101
DRIFTING	102
GONE	103

Dedication

This book is dedicated to the congregations who have challenged me to share my understanding of faith, and especially those seniors to whom I seem young!

Why this book?

More than fifty years ago, Michel Quoist wrote:

> If we knew how to listen to God, if we knew how to look around us, our whole life would become prayer. ... Words are only a means. However, the silent prayer which has moved beyond words must always spring from everyday life, for everyday life is the raw material of prayer.[1]

If we seek God, we will see Him revealed in the people and events in our lives.

Including seniors. The things that the seniors and the elderly do and say and think and feel can challenge us to think about faith; reveal God to us; and teach us about our relationship with our Eternal Father/Mother.

That is the purpose of this book. As you read these reflections, it is likely they will conjure familiar images for you. I hope they will also help you to meditate on God and your relationship with Him.

This is not a book to be read from cover to cover. It is designed to be dipped into, sequentially or not, with favourite passages revisited from time to time. Perhaps it will inspire you to add your own reflections on the theme.

---

[1] Michel Quoist, *Prayers of life*, MH Gill and Sons Ltd, Dublin, 1963, p. 22.

Why seniors?

From my youth, I have always admired seniors—their presence, their wisdom, their acceptance of life. And their faith—their commitment to continue the journey of faith despite all the difficulties they have faced and are facing. As a young man I enjoyed the company and the wisdom of seniors.

My own parents reached ages of 90 and 106. Nowadays, I'm a senior too!

In this book, I share the inspiration I receive from seniors, and also faith seen through the eyes of seniors. So, hopefully, these reflections will inspire you no matter what your age.

My life has been blessed by seniors. My faith has been inspired by seniors. I hope I can share some of that blessing and inspiration through this book.

A word about Biblical quotes

A Biblical quote is included for each reflection—yet I do this with a little discomfort. It is too easy to extract verses from their context where they have a particular meaning, and to use them to convey another meaning in a different context. It is possible I have done that in this book—not to give credibility, but to help you to delve into the Bible and to seek out its truth. Forgive me if I've been simplistic. If the Biblical references are helpful, explore them; if not, ignore them.

Contemporary translations have been used. All are available (free of charge) online from various sites.

Bible Translations quoted:

Scripture quotations marked **NIV** are taken from *The Holy Bible: New International Version®*, NIV® Copyright © 1973, 1978, 1984, 2011 by Biblica, Inc.® Used by permission. All rights reserved worldwide.

Scripture quotations marked **GNT** are taken from *Good News Translation®* (Today's English Version, Second Edition), Copyright © 1992 American Bible Society. All rights reserved.

Scripture quotations marked **MSG** are taken from *The Message*. Copyright © 1993, 1994, 1995, 1996, 2000, 2001, 2002. Used by permission of NavPress Publishing Group.

Scripture quotations marked **TLB** are from *The Living Bible* copyright © 1971 by Tyndale House Foundation. Used by permission of Tyndale House Publishers Inc., Carol Stream, Illinois 60188. All rights reserved.

SENIORS THROUGH THEIR OWN EYES

DIGNITY

There is little dignity in ageing, Father.

We are the butt of jokes
    about forgetfulness,
    posture,
    clothing,
    wrinkles,
    hearing,
    incontinence—
And many of them are true.
We ask,
    'What did he say?'
    'Can you open this for me?'
    'What do I have to do?'
    'Do I know her?'

We are prodded,
    and measured,
    and sampled,
    and questioned
By medical practitioners of every ilk,
Who seem fascinated about
    our blood,
    our urine,
    our bowels,
    our eating,
    our exercise,
    our state of mind.

And we accept it,
    walking the corridors of medical facilities
        in gowns that leave our unattractive features
        exposed;
    allowing doctors
        to access our intimate body parts;
    making messes
        which others clean up;
    accepting help with basic activities.
It's not that others want to humiliate us.
They seek only to help.
It's just that I feel my dignity went …
    well …
        wherever it was they took my clothes.

And then, Father, I remember:
That Jesus died an undignified death—
    mocked,
    beaten,
    taunted,
    betrayed—
By choice,
Without protest—
For me.
How can I say thank you?

This is the kind of life you've been invited into, the kind of life Christ lived. He suffered everything that came his way so you would know that it could be done, and also know how to do it, step-by-step. (1 Peter 2: 21, MSG)

BIRTHDAYS

It's my birthday, Father.

Birthdays matter.
The more we have, it seems,
    the longer we live!
When we are old,
Each may be our last,
So every birthday is a 'big one',
Every anniversary a celebration of endurance.

We gather with family,
We blow out candles,
We eat cake,
We open gifts,
We tell stories about the past,
And we muse about the future.

The older I get,
The more I recall of your goodness,
The more of your blessings I give thanks for,
The more of your love I celebrate.

I don't know how many more birthdays I will have,
Father.
It doesn't matter.
Thank you for what I have had,
And what I now have.

Yes, we should make the most of what God gives, both the bounty and the capacity to enjoy it, accepting what's given and delighting in the work. It's God's gift! God deals out joy in the present, the now. It's useless to brood over how long we might live. (Ecclesiastes 5: 19–20, MSG)

YOU CAN'T DIE

She forbade me to die, Father.

You can't die, she said.
When I'm grown,
When my children are growing,
I will always need you.
I will always need
    your help,
    your advice,
    your company,
    your smile,
    your love …
You!

I laughed—
Not unkindly,
But to bring perspective.
Of course I will die.
She knows it,
I know it.
I hope she outlives me.

Help me, Father, to prepare her:
To teach her about you,
To help her to find you,
So that when I am gone,
She will know that you will be here.

Only be careful, and watch yourselves closely so that you do not forget the things your eyes have seen or let them fade from your heart as long as you live. Teach them to your children and to their children after them. (Deuteronomy 4: 9, NIV)

HEAVEN

I'm confused by heaven, Father.

So much of the Bible is metaphor,
And I don't see much logic these days
In a heaven filled with
    mansions,
    streets of gold,
    pearly gates.
Perhaps I'd prefer
    plush carpet,
    air conditioning,
    reliable internet connection.

Of course, heaven is you, Father,
    your presence,
    your company,
    your nearness;
The chance to chat,
To give thanks,
To honour you—
Simply, to be with you.

That will do.
That will be heaven for me.

Paul wrote: We are not our own bosses to live or die as we ourselves might choose. Living or dying we follow the Lord. Either way we are his. Christ died and rose again for this very purpose, so that he can be our Lord both while we live and when we die. (Romans 14: 7-9, TLB)

DOTAGE

Can I share a rhyme with you, Father?

I read,
'In my dotage I've become
Inert, defunct, inane.
Oh to be like yesteryear:
Ert, funct and ane again.'[2]
Do you like that,
Or have you heard it before?

Sometimes I feel
That my use-by date has expired;
That I am of no further use;
That I am simply occupying a chair in a waiting room
    until my turn comes.

Once I was needed.
I helped with the grand-children—
    but now the young ones have grown.
I helped at church fetes—
    but now I'm expected to sit and drink tea.
I offered advice—
    but now my knowledge is considered out of date.

---

[2] Source unknown.

Is this how it is to be, Father?
Are there things still waiting for me to do?
And will I see them when you show them to me?

You have taught me ever since I was young, and I still tell of your wonderful acts. Now that I am old and my hair is grey, do not abandon me, O God! Be with me while I proclaim your power and might to all generations to come. (Psalm 71: 17–18, GNT)

PILLOW

I'm fond of my pillow, Father.

That sounds silly,
But when I want to sleep,
My pillow is just right.

It wasn't expensive:
It's one of millions.
It even gets changed regularly.
But it feels right—
It's familiar,
And it's mine.

Where do you rest when you tire of the world?

What am I saying?
You never grow tired,
You never rest,
You always care for me,
Giving me rest
So I can face a new day.

Don't you know? Haven't you heard? The Lord is the everlasting God; he created all the world. He never grows tired or weary. No one understands his thoughts. (Isaiah 40: 28, GNT)

BALD

What happened to my hair, Father?

As a young man,
I had a full head of hair,
    dark,
    shiny,
    worth running fingers through.
But over the years,
It disappeared,
Apparently seeking greener pastures.

Once you numbered the hairs on my head—
Now you probably name them,
Because you care for me
That much.

Aren't five sparrows sold for two pennies? Yet not one sparrow is forgotten by God. Even the hairs of your head have all been counted. So do not be afraid; you are worth much more than many sparrows! (Luke 12: 6–7, GNT)

CHANGING VALUES

I am uncomfortable with the changing values, Father.

People don't marry—
    they raise children with their 'partner'.
Obscenities are accepted as normal conversation—
    and they proliferate on television programs.
It is assumed that any date
    is followed by sex.
Drug taking and excessive alcohol
    are dismissed with humour by comedians.
Violence is seen as an appropriate response
    if we are offended,
    cut off in traffic,
    or just wanting to express our feelings!
The old coward principles are ignored—
    don't hit a man when he is down,
    one at a time,
    pick on someone your own size.

I could go on, Father
(You know I often do)
But I am troubled.
I didn't know it would be like this—
    that society would change so much;
    that the values I grew up with would be lost;
    that the behaviour I was taught would be
    outmoded;

that your word would be discarded by many;
that your teachings would be scorned;
that your sacrifice and your love would be rejected.

Of course, I couldn't know.
But could I have made a difference?
Did I make a difference?
Am I making a difference?
Will I continue to make a difference—
    perhaps not to the world,
    but to my small corner of it?

What can I do, Father?
What can I?
What?

A voice of one calling in the wilderness, 'Prepare the way for the Lord, make straight paths for him.' (Matthew 3: 3, NIV)

HALO

I have a halo, Father.

My passport photo
    was taken against a white screen.
My face alone is visible—
My white hair and white beard
Forming a halo,
    against the background.

I assume I'll be recognised from my photo
    if I need to be,
But the halo is an unlikely touch:
Not something I deserve;
Something reserved for angels,
Or, according to artists,
For your son
And his earthly mother.

And yet,
You care for humankind.
Among all your creation,
You honour us.
Even without the halo,
Am I worthy, Father?

When I look at the sky, which you have made, at the moon and the stars, which you set in their places—what are human beings, that you think of them; mere mortals, that you care for them? Yet you made them inferior only to yourself; you crowned them with glory and honour. (Psalm 8: 3–5, GNT)

SENSES

My senses are fading, Father.

I struggle to hear
    the voices of grandchildren;
    the dialogue on the television;
    the gentle sounds of the wind;
    the uplifting calls of birds;
So a hearing aid helps me to hear.

I struggle to see
    the fine print of a newspaper;
    the text of a book;
    the photos I love to peruse;
    the cricket ball on the television;
So spectacles help me to see.

As I'm ageing,
I am losing sensitivity in my senses, Father;
But let me never lose my ability
    to see you at work,
    and to hear your voice—
In the world,
And in my life.

Jesus told them, 'Go back and tell John what's going on: The blind see, the lame walk, lepers are cleansed, the deaf hear, the dead are raised, the wretched of the earth learn that God is on their side. Is this what you were expecting? Then count yourselves most blessed!' (Matthew 4: 4–6, MSG)

APPEARANCE

I'm shocked at my appearance, Father.

My face has changed.
It's not just the proliferation of wrinkles,
But my cheeks and chin and jowls and neck
    have sagged and drooped and puffed.
My hair—what's left
    is grey—or perhaps white—and lifeless.
My posture is stooped.
My confident stride has been reduced to a shuffle,
    to instinctively protect myself from falling.
What happened?
And when?
I barely recognise my reflection.

You don't look on the outside, Father,
But the inside,
And I'm grateful—
Or I think I am.

What do you see when you look at me—
Not at my outside, but at my inside?
Do you still recognise
    my faith,
    my service,
    my desire to honour you?
Am I still attractive to you
On the inside?

But the Lord said to him, 'Pay no attention to how tall and handsome he is. I have rejected him, because I do not judge as people judge. They look at the outward appearance, but I look at the heart.' (1 Samuel 16: 7, GNT)

LOST GRANDCHILDREN

I don't see the grandkids anymore, Father.

It breaks my heart.
My son and his wife split up,
And the children went with their Mum,
And she doesn't want to see me,
Or want them to see me.
She has 'moved on' with her life,
And others are left struggling in the wake.

I don't know what tore their marriage apart.
I'm sure that she alone wasn't to blame.
But why must the children be torn away
    from all they know
    and all they love?
And why must they be lost to me,
Never to see them,
    to watch them grow,
    to delight in their achievements,
    to admire who they become?
It's not fair, Father.

Do you feel the same way, Father,
When parents tear their children away from you,
Or simply discourage them from knowing you?
And do you cry too?

If anyone should cause one of these little ones to lose his faith in me, it would be better for that person to have a large millstone tied around his neck and be drowned in the deep sea. (Matthew 18: 6, GNT)

CHECK UP

Will I live another year, Father?

That's what I ask my doctor,
Each year around my birthday
When I have a check-up.
He checks blood pressure,
    and heart rhythm,
Arranges blood tests,
Asks about my health,
    my state of mind.
And I ask,
So will I make it to my next birthday?
He smiles.
God knows.

You know.
It's enough, Father.
I don't need to know how or when.
It's enough to know that you are here—
Wherever and whenever 'here' may be,
And you are there—
Wherever and whenever 'there' may be …
Waiting for me.

Yes, we should make the most of what God gives, both the bounty and the capacity to enjoy it, accepting what's given and delighting in the work. It's God's gift! God deals out joy in the present, the now. It's useless to brood over how long we might live. (Ecclesiastes 5: 19–20, MSG)

ELDERLY

Am I elderly, Father?

The media reported an incident involving
   an elderly man.
Their tone was sympathetic,
Even compassionate,
Sensitively implying that he was
   vulnerable,
   frail,
   unable to cope with trauma,
   lacking resilience.

I should have appreciated the journalist's tone—
But the 'elderly man' was younger than me!

Is that how others see me, Father?
Is that how you see me?
I admit my body is weakening.
I can do most of what I always did,
But it takes longer
And hurts more!

I want to stay young in my faith—
Mature in my understanding,
But young in my willingness to serve;
Young in my ability to adapt to new situations;

Young in my confidence to speak for you,
    and to share my faith with others.
Keep me young, Father.

He fills my life with good things, so that I stay young and strong like an eagle. (Psalm 103: 5, GNT)

US AND ME

It was 'us', Father. Now it's 'me'.

I can barely remember when it was just me—
The first eighteen years;
Then it was us.
Even before we married,
It was us.
No decision,
No event,
No thought
Was for me—
It was always for us.

A lifetime of being invited to events jointly;
Signing documents jointly;
Purchasing a home jointly;
Holding bank accounts jointly;
Making decisions jointly;
Even shopping jointly.

And now it's just me.
Alone.
One.
And it's hard, Father.
I haven't the strength to be one;
I haven't the wisdom to be one;
I haven't the heart to be one;
I want to be *us* again.

It will take time, Father.
Be patient with me.

Turn to me, Lord, and be merciful to me, because I am lonely and weak. Relieve me of my worries and save me from all my troubles. (Psalm 25: 16–17, GNT)

FUNERALS

I'm tired of funerals, Father.

It seems that is my main entertainment these days—
The only time I go out.
I go because these are my friends,
    my peers,
    my cohort.
We learnt together,
    worked together,
    raised kids together,
    worshipped together,
    relaxed together.

I cannot desert them now:
Even in death,
I want to honour them—
    to honour their lives,
    to honour their memory,
    to honour their impact on my life.

But attendance at these events is diminishing.
Of course, their family is there,
And those who want to support the family,
But there are few of the old crowd present.

Will there be anyone left to attend my funeral,
To honour my life and my memory?

Blessed are the poor in spirit, for theirs is the kingdom of heaven. Blessed are those who mourn, for they will be comforted. (Matthew 5: 3–4, NIV)

OCCASIONAL VISITS

I miss my grand-kids, Father.

It's no-one's fault.
We live some way apart,
    and we struggle to get there,
    and they struggle to get here.
Our lives are busy.
There are other things drag on our time.

But I want to see how they are growing,
To hear of their new achievements,
To know the things that interest them,
To understand their evolving character,
To enjoy their vibrant energy,
And to share the things that delight them.

Do you feel that way about me, Father,
When I don't keep in touch,
When there's a gap between my visits
With you?

Turn to the Lord and pray to him, now that he is near.
(Isaiah 55: 6, GNT)

LEGACY

People keep talking about their legacy, Father.

They want to leave their mark;
To have something of themselves remain
When they are gone from this life.

Me? Not so much.
People will remember me
The way they choose to remember me;
Their memories will be cluttered
With my trivial, humorous and embarrassing moments,
As much as my deep and meaningful achievements.
My legacy will be what they make it,
Not what I deem it.

Help me to live this life, Father,
In such a way
That my life makes a difference
Here,
Now.

When they see me waiting, expecting your Word, those who fear you will take heart and be glad. I can see now, God, that your decisions are right; your testing has taught me what's true and right. Oh, love me—and right now!—hold me tight! just the way you promised. Now comfort me so I can live, really live; your revelation is the tune I dance to. (Psalm 119: 74–77, MSG)

SENIORS THROUGH YOUNGER EYES

JOY

I love their joy, Father.

When we go out together as a family;
When we eat a meal together;
When we watch a movie;
When we celebrate a birthday;
When we open Christmas presents;
When we just talk ...
There is joy.

Sometimes we hear stories from their past,
Snippets which give insight into their lives.
It hasn't been easy,
Yet they have retained the joy.

It is *your* joy they exude:
Joy which is not dependent on circumstances,
But joy which comes from your Spirit
Within.

Thank you for joy, Father.

All you that are righteous, shout for joy for what the Lord has done; praise him, all you that obey him. (Psalm 33 :1, GNT)

SONGS

She remembers the songs he sang her, Father.

Although he is no longer with her,
She thinks of him,
And she sings—
Smiling as she recalls the tunes and the words.

Her memory misses so much,
But not this.
Every song is word perfect,
Every note as true as her wavering voice can make it.

What love was theirs.
What memories are hers.

What will I remember when I am old, Father?
Will I recall songs of love?
Will I recall songs of you?
When all else fades from my memory, Father,
Let me always remember you.

I will remember your great deeds, Lord; I will recall the wonders you did in the past. (Psalm 77: 11, GNT)

SITTING

I need to be less busy, Father.

He was retired.
I was making conversation.
What do you do with your day? I asked.
Sometimes it's good to do nothing, he said.

I didn't understand—
Boredom does not settle easily on me.
I need to be busy,
Flitting from one thing to another,
Filling my day
    with people,
    activity,
    life.

Sometimes it's good to do nothing.
I tried it.
It took time for me to learn to take time—
    to reflect,
    to think,
    to look,
    to listen—
And he's right.

Am I too busy, Father?

Phil Ridden   *Reflections on faith inspired by seniors*

Do I fill my life with so much activity,
That I miss your presence,
    miss your availability?
I often pray that I will see you
    in all the events of my life,
But do I miss your gentle whisper?

The Lord said, 'Go out and stand on the mountain in the presence of the Lord, for the Lord is about to pass by.' Then a great and powerful wind tore the mountains apart and shattered the rocks before the Lord, but the Lord was not in the wind. After the wind there was an earthquake, but the Lord was not in the earthquake. After the earthquake came a fire, but the Lord was not in the fire. And after the fire came a gentle whisper. (I Kings 19: 11–12, NIV)

DRIVING

I worry about him driving, Father.

He passed his latest test;
He operates the car satisfactorily;
He makes good judgements;
And yet ...
How will he cope in a crisis?
How will he respond to the unexpected?
How will he adapt to changing conditions?

He doesn't go out much.
He could call a taxi;
He could take a bus;
But then he would be admitting
That he has lost his independence,
That he is no longer in change of his life.

Is that how you feel about me, Father?
I want to be independent,
    in charge of my life,
        confident to make good judgements,
        able to cope in a crisis,
        able to respond to the unexpected,
        able to adapt to the change.
But you know my weaknesses.

You know how often I fail—
    fail to live what I profess,
    fail to serve you as I ought,
    fail to take the opportunities you give me,
    fail you.

Sit beside me—
Always,
As I motor through life.

He guides me in the right paths, as he has promised.
(Psalm 23: 3, GNT)

BLIND

She cannot see, Father.

There may be a tunnel of light
Entering her eyes,
But she is effectively blind;
Yet she lives life with confidence.

She moves around her home,
    rides on buses,
    visits friends,
    even goes shopping,
Without seeing clearly.

She gets it wrong sometimes:
    rides the wrong bus,
    finds herself in an unknown location,
    buys the wrong item;
But she lives by faith—
    faith in what she knows,
    faith in the life she knows,
    faith in the kindness of others,
    and faith that you will always be there.

I envy her faith, Father.
Sometimes what I see distracts me,
So that I rely upon my own abilities,
And not on you.

Help me to live a life of confidence,
Of faith
In you.

For our life is a matter of faith, not of sight. (2 Corinthians 5: 7, GNT).

YELLING

I have to yell at him, Father.

Because he struggles to hear,
I must speak loudly to him;
And because he struggles to hear,
He speaks loudly to me,
With no sense of how loud he is.

It's embarrassing,
Because our conversation is amplified
For all around to hear—
Even those things that are personal.

It's tiring,
Because I am uncertain of our communication,
Unsure what he has heard
And what he has missed.

It's frustrating,
Because I have things I want him to understand,
But I struggle to receive clear feedback
That shows that he comprehends.

But it's not his fault,
So I try to be patient with him.

Are you like that with me, Father?
Are you patient with my deafness?
So often
I struggle to hear your voice,
Your words of direction,
> or comfort,
> or healing,
> or instruction,
> or wisdom.

Speak to me as he and I do, Father.
Yell at me—
Use a megaphone if need be.
For I am sometimes deaf to your voice,
But I want to hear you.

Doing something for you, bringing something to you—that's not what you're after. Being religious, acting pious—that's not what you're asking for. You've opened my ears so I can listen. (Psalm 40: 6, MSG)

COMPLAINING

He's always complaining, Father.

They wake him when he wants to sleep;
They shower him according to their schedule;
The food is not hot;
He doesn't like corned beef;
His bed wasn't made properly;
Someone has stolen his bananas;
The lady in the next room keeps him awake;
The air-conditioning is too cold …
The list is endless.

No matter what they do,
Or we do,
He is not happy.
His world is not as he wants it;
And it's their fault,
　　someone's fault,
　　　our fault …

Who am I to comment?
This could be me—
Always complaining:
I am not happy.
The world is not as I want it,
And it's their fault,
　　someone's fault,
　　　your fault …

Phil Ridden   *Reflections on faith inspired by seniors*   45

You didn't answer my prayers;
A good man suffered;
Those who oppose you are succeeding in their plans;
You allowed people to die in the tsunami;
Your servant has been martyred;
My friend wasn't healed;
I missed out on that promotion;
You didn't tell me what I should do …

I complain with the best of them.
Yet you love me.

Does a clay pot dare argue with its maker, a pot that is like all the others? Does the clay ask the potter what he is doing? Does the pot complain that its maker has no skill? (Isaiah 45: 9, GNT)

Complain if you must, but don't lash out. Keep your mouth shut, and let your heart do the talking. Build your case before God and wait for his verdict. (Psalm 4: 4–5, MSG)

NAPPIES

It's a delicate topic, Father,

He wears nappies,
And it embarrasses him.
At the end of life
He revisits the beginning of life—
    fed by others,
    helped with dressing,
    never leaving home without a carer …
And wearing nappies.

But I love that his faith has reverted too.
No longer
    challenging,
    questioning,
    analysing,
    struggling to understand and rationalise and
    interpret …
His is the faith of a child—
Simply trusting,
Simply confident in your love,
Simply assured that whatever lies ahead,
    this side of death or the other,
You will be there.

Teach me that faith, Father.

For I am certain that nothing can separate us from his love: neither death nor life, neither angels nor other heavenly rulers or powers, neither the present nor the future, neither the world above nor the world below—there is nothing in all creation that will ever be able to separate us from the love of God which is ours through Christ Jesus our Lord. (Romans 8: 38–39, GNT)

FRIENDSHIP

She showed such dedication to a friend, Father.

He was confined to bed for years;
The consequence of a stroke.
And despite her own ageing
She visited him every week—
Not as partner or lover,
Just as friend.

What a friendship,
To stand by him,
    visit him,
    talk to him,
    read to him,
    hold his hand,
Every week
For years.

You do that for me, Father.
In the intimate companionship of your Spirit,
You are not just beside me each week,
But always with me,
Always within me,
Always.

I will ask the Father, and he will give you another Helper, who will stay with you forever. He is the Spirit, who reveals the truth about God. The world cannot receive him, because it cannot see him or know him. But you know him, because he remains with you and is in you. (John 14: 16–17, GNT)

GRIEF

He mourns his wife, Father.

The only love of his life,
The ever-present,
Always reliable,
Love of his life,
Now gone—
And he is lost.
He weeps for her,
And he weeps for himself,
Struggling to make a life
Without her.

That's how life would be for me, Father,
If I lost you.
I would weep for myself,
And struggle to make a life
Without you.

I know you'll never leave me—
But when I feel alone, hold me;
When I feel deserted, comfort me.
When I feel lost, take me by the hand and lead me.

Live content with what you have, for you always have God's presence. For hasn't he promised you, 'I will never leave you alone, never! And I will not loosen my grip on your life!' (Hebrews 13: 5, NIV)

HOSPITAL

She's in hospital again, Father.

The bones are brittle;
The heart is sputtering;
The organs are failing;
The skin is decaying.
It is the way of humanity—
    we age,
    we tire,
    we die.
She knows it and I know it.

Yet there is life still:
The heart beats;
The mind thinks;
The will strives.

Father, hold her when I'm not there.
Take her hand in yours.
Place your arms around her shoulders.
Give her your strength,
    your courage,
    your peace.

Don't panic. I'm with you. There's no need to fear for I'm your God. I'll give you strength. I'll help you. I'll hold you steady, keep a firm grip on you. (Isaiah 41: 9–10, MSG)

TELEVISION

She watches a lot of television, Father.

Confined to her room,
Unable to get out much,
    except in the occasional care of others,
Television shows her what is happening
In the wider world,
Beyond the confines of her room.

Her view,
Her understanding of the world,
Is defined for her by the media:
    selected,
    explained,
    reviewed;
Through the coloured lenses of others.

Yet …
Perhaps I'm the same, Father.
I see the world
Through the lenses of those I choose I follow,
    those I choose to listen to,
    those I choose to believe;
Through the coloured lenses of others.

Do I follow the right people, Father,
Or do I allow myself to be drawn away from you
By those I choose to listen to?

He quoted a proverb: 'Can a blind man guide a blind man?' Wouldn't they both end up in the ditch? An apprentice doesn't lecture the master. The point is to be careful who you follow as your teacher. (Luke 6: 39–40, MSG)

GENERATION

They saw so much, Father, this generation.

They lived so much;
They endured so much;
They adapted to so much—
World war,
Economic depression and other financial crises;
Terrorism;
Pandemic;
The advent of motor cars,
    air travel,
    radio and television,
    telephone,
    supermarkets,
    artificial fabrics and plastics;
The computer chip, with its impact
    on shopping,
    banking,
    communication,
    information …

It's been an astounding century or so,
And these old folk,
Whom we so often dismiss
    as frail and incompetent and reactionary,
Have lived it—
Embraced the innovations,
Adjusted to the changes.

Make me adaptable, Father.
Enable me to embrace
    new understandings of you,
    new ways to glorify you,
    new expressions of faith,
    new opportunities to serve.
Make me new every day.

But the Lord says, 'Do not cling to events of the past or dwell on what happened long ago. Watch for the new thing I am going to do. It is happening already—you can see it now!' (Isaiah 43: 18–19, GNT)

GOODBYE

Each time we say goodbye may be the last, Father.

I know that.
I think he knows it too.

We enjoy our time together,
Talking,
Or just sitting,
As old friends who do not need words
As evidence of companionship.

But we know that it will come to an end
Any day now.
He speaks less;
He tires more quickly.

We say goodbye,
Knowing that it may be the last time.

Thank you, Father,
That we never have to say goodbye to you.
That you will leave us
Alone.

May the Lord our God be with us as he was with our ancestors; may he never leave us nor forsake us. (1 Kings 8: 57, NIV)

DAILY PHONE CALL

They phone each other every day, Father.

They are siblings,
    each ageing,
    each living alone,
    each vulnerable to falls and health crises;
So they phone each other every day,
At the same time,
Just to check.
Week about, they take turns at initiating the call—
Unless the call does not come,
Or the call is not answered.

I imagine you to be like that, Father.
Do you check on me every day,
Just to make sure I'm OK—
Not just in my body,
But in my faith?
And if I don't answer,
Will you come near
And breathe your life into my heart?

He is near to those who call to him, who call to him with sincerity. (Psalm 145: 18, GNT)

PLAYFUL

He can't be old, Father, because he is still playful.

Despite his advancing years,
There is still a child within him:
A playful spirit
That wants to laugh
And be silly.

I love that spirit.
I remember it from when I was a child.
We rolled down hillsides,
    built hill trolleys,
    hid from one another,
    went on adventures,
    ran in circles,
    hung upside down from climbing frames …

That playful spirit is
    creative,
    fun-loving,
    energetic,
    resilient,
    generous,
    hopeful.

Give me a playful spirit
In my faith—
To seek new ways to spread your word;
To express the joy which your love brings;
To be energised by serving you;
To bounce back from disappointment and trauma;
To be generous in my dealings with others;
To be full of hope for this life and the next.

I assure you that whoever does not receive the Kingdom of God like a child will never enter it. (Mark 10: 15, GNT)

SLIPPING AWAY

She is losing touch, Father.

Day by day,
Week by week,
Month by month,
We see her awareness diminishing,
Her mind and memory slipping away.

She is unsure where she is,
    or who we are,
    or what she is doing,
    or what she should expect.

At times she is aware of her unawareness
And it agitates her.
At other times she is unaware
Of her disconnection with reality.

You are my reality, Father.
I know that
Little by little,
Day by day,
Week by week,
Month by month,
I could lose touch with you;
My awareness of your presence diminishing,
My faith slipping away.

Phil Ridden   *Reflections on faith inspired by seniors*

Keep me connected.

Stay in my thinking;
Stay in my understanding;
Stay in my actions;
Stay in my ambitions;
Stay in my dreams.
Stay in my life—
And let me know your presence.

As I lie in bed, I remember you; all night long I think of you, because you have always been my help. In the shadow of your wings I sing for joy. I cling to you, and your hand keeps me safe. (Psalm 63: 6–8, GNT)

SINGING

She still plays piano, Father.

So much has been lost from her memory:
Who she was,
Where she is,
Who she knows,
How to care for herself.

And yet,
She sits at the piano
And plays
And sings.
Sometimes the words are lost,
But most are there.

How is it that
Amid the confusion of her mind,
Some things remain clear?

I'd like my mind to be like that, Father—
Not with music—
(It was never there)—
but with you.

When my memory weakens,
When I am confused,

Help me to recall
   your love,
   your faithfulness,
   your generosity,
   your forgiveness.
Let it flash like a neon sign
Through the mist of my mind.

Hallelujah! You who serve God, praise God! Just to speak his name is praise! Just to remember God is a blessing—now and tomorrow and always. From east to west, from dawn to dusk, keep lifting all your praises to God! (Psalm 113: 1–3, MSG)

WISDOM

The wisdom of the aged is a cliché, Father.

It's a cliché,
But there's truth to it.

I love to hear their stories:
    stories generated by years of experience,
    stories inspired by a moment,
    stories created in pain or joy,
    stories crafted with the care of a poet.

Their wisdom is simple:
Not lost in academic jargon,
    excessive analysis,
    or complex exposition;
But told as it is or as it was,
    unadorned,
    authentic.
I can see the narrative
Unfolding behind their eyes
As they recall each event and recount it.

They make no demands,
No ambitious claims
    of insight.
It's up to me to sift and glean
That which brings clarity to me.

Phil Ridden   *Reflections on faith inspired by seniors*

Solomon sought wisdom;
I'd like to say that I do too:
But
    sometimes
I'm more intent on sharing my wisdom,
Than hearing the wisdom of others.

You are the source of all wisdom.
Make me a learner.

Start with God—the first step in learning is bowing down to God; only fools thumb their noses at such wisdom and learning. (Proverbs 1: 7, MSG)

FAÇADE

I want to look deeper, Father.

I want to see
Behind the façade of
    white hair,
    wrinkled face,
    cloudy eyes,
    silver hearing aid,
    compressed neck,
    arthritic hands,
    stooped back,
    lumbering walk …

All the signs of ageing, Father,
Distract me,
Tempt me into prejudice and stereotypical assumptions
About old folk.

Her senses may be failing,
Her speed of response may be slowing,
Her flexibility may be stiffening—
But there is life in the eyes,
    playfulness in the mind,
    compassion in the heart.

Phil Ridden   *Reflections on faith inspired by seniors*

You do not love us less when our bodies grow weak.
You do not listen to us any less when our words slow down.
You do not understand us any less when our mind is confused.

Ancient of days,
You know about age.
Help me to see beyond the façade,
To love and to learn from all,
Regardless of age.

Do not cast me away when I am old; do not forsake me when my strength is gone. (Psalm 71: 9, NIV)

NOT THERE YET

It was his eightieth birthday, Father.

I said:
'Some say there is a climactic moment in our lives,
    a pivotal moment,
    a moment which defines us,
    and sets us on a path to the future.
When was it for you?'
And he answered,
'I don't know—
    I haven't had it yet!'

Eighty years,
And still anticipating
    great moments,
    exciting events,
    challenging opportunities;
Still claiming time
    for new experiences,
    new challenges,
    new thoughts.
The future still called him,
    still offered him unknown treasures,
    still held out its hands,
    still promised adventure.

I am so much younger,
Yet I am tempted to settle,
To sit back and let life cruise by.

I want to always look forward, Father.
I want to hope for what is ahead,
    not mourn what is behind.
I want to continue to enjoy life fulfilling,
    not gradually diminishing fulfilment.
I want to be inspired by your power and your love,
    not disheartened by my own inhibited perspective.
I want to enjoy life eternal,
    not life limited and truncated.

Am I making the most of your offer, Father?
Am I living the fulfilled life you gave me?
Am I still running towards the goal?
Hold out your hands to me
And lead me into the future—
No matter how old I am.
What do you have next for me, Father?
I'm ready.
Let's do it!

I'm not saying that I have this all together, that I have it made. But I am well on my way, reaching out for Christ, who has so wondrously reached out for me. Friends, don't get me wrong: By no means do I count myself an expert in all of this, but I've got my eye on the goal, where God is beckoning us onward—to Jesus. I'm off and running, and I'm not turning back. (Philippians 3: 12–14, MSG)

WALKING FRAME

She needs help to walk now, Father.

She had a walking stick for a while.
Now she uses a frame to
> alert her to obstacles which would trip her up;
> assist her to maintain her balance over difficult terrain;
> steady her when she feels uncertain;
> help her to carry her baggage;
> lean on when she is tired.

I need help in my walk too, Father—
> my faith walk.

I need you to
> alert me to obstacles which would trip me up;
> assist me to maintain my balance over difficult circumstances;
> steady me when I feel uncertain;
> help me to carry my baggage and burdens;
> lean on when I am tired.

Come to me, all you who are weary and burdened, and I will give you rest. (Matthew 11: 28, NIV)

BLOCKED EARS

He didn't want to know, Father.

The doctor tried to explain
What needed to be done,
And the consequences if it was not,
But he didn't want to hear.

I understand.
He has been through so much,
Suffered so long,
And now he wants peace.
What he doesn't hear he need not deal with,
So, like a child,
He puts his fingers in his ears.

Do I do that, Father?
When I don't want to hear,
When I fear your call,
When I worry about what you might want of me—
Do I put my fingers in my ears?

Your ears are open but you don't hear a thing. Your eyes are awake but you don't see a thing. The people are blockheads! They stick their fingers in their ears so they won't have to listen; They screw their eyes shut so they won't have to look, so they won't have to deal with me face-to-face and let me heal them. But you have God-blessed eyes—eyes that see! And God-blessed ears—ears that hear! (Matthew 13: 14–16, MSG)

STRUGGLING

It's wrong that they struggle, Father.

They have spent a lifetime,
Raising a family;
Giving all they had to help their children
    become what they wanted to be;
Supporting their children through difficult times;
Baby-sitting grand-children;
Caring for neighbours and friends;
Offering comfort and companionship,
    and money and gifts
Whenever they could,
And whenever it was needed.

And now,
They struggle:
Drinking cheap tea and coffee
    because that's all they can afford;
Rugged against the cold
    because electricity costs are rising;
Sitting in broken chairs with creaking springs
    because they have no capital for updates;
Taking a bus to hospital to visit their beloved
    because they cannot afford the taxi;
Hunting for bargains and home brands and economies.

These folk
Who were always available to help others,
Always willing to share what they had,
Are now struggling to make ends meet.

It's not right, Father—
But nor is idle complaint.
Show me how to help.
Show me how to love.

'When, Lord, did we ever see you hungry and feed you, or thirsty and give you a drink? When did we ever see you a stranger and welcome you in our homes, or naked and clothe you? When did we ever see you sick or in prison, and visit you?' The King will reply, 'I tell you, whenever you did this for one of the least important of these followers of mine, you did it for me!' (Matthew 25: 37–40, GNT)

GIVING BACK

His is a life of service, Father.

'When you retire,
You give back, don't you?' he said.

'You spend your life,
    working,
    accumulating,
    thriving,
For yourself and your family.
Then, when you retire,
You give back,' he said.

'Money matters less,
Time matters less,
Future matters less,
So you use your time,
And your accumulated knowledge and skills,
And maybe a bit of wisdom,
To help others,' he said.

'It doesn't matter where.
Everywhere you look
There are people who need your help:
    gentle labour,
    advice,

    encouragement,
    companionship,
    conversation …
So you help others;
You give them the gift of your time—
You give back,' he said.

Do I give back, Father?
Even now,
Though not yet retired,
I could give back.
Will I be able to see the need?
Will I be willing to respond?

Each of you should use whatever gift you have received to serve others, as faithful stewards of God's grace in its various forms. (1 Peter 4: 10, NIV)

ANGER

What do I do with the anger, Father?

She's gone;
Passed into your care.
But I am left
With things I shouldn't have said,
    and things I should have;
Things I shouldn't have done,
    and things I should have.

Our relationship wasn't always easy.
It was her fault,
And it was mine.
She was unkind,
And so was I.
She should have,
    could have,
    might have,
    perhaps would have,
But didn't—
    and nor did I.

Father forgive me
For the hurt I caused.
Heal the hurt
That she caused.

Replace my hurt,
>   my tears,
>   my regrets,
With peace—
Your peace.

Oh, that my steps might be steady, keeping to the course you set; Then I'd never have any regrets in comparing my life with your counsel. (Psalm 119: 5–6, MSG)

NEW HIPS

He has new hips, Father.

It's remarkable:
The old joints were worn,
Grinding together painfully,
So they were replaced by new joints,
Fashioned from metal.
Now he walks confidently,
    evenly,
    smartly.

Will you, Father,
    replace the damaged parts of my life like that—
The parts of my character which are faulty,
That grind against others?

God, make a fresh start in me, shape a Genesis week from the chaos of my life. (Psalm 51: 10, MSG)

RESILIENCE

I love his resilience, Father.

He goes to hospital regularly,
For yet another failing.
If he was a car, I'd trade him in!
What will go wrong next?

Yet each time I bring him home,
He is full of life.
He laughs.
He can't wait to see people.
There is the hint of a spring in his stagger!

Give me a faith like that, Father.
When my faith weakens,
When it fails me,
Renew me,
Strengthen me,
To trust again,
And to serve you with vigour.

But they that wait upon the Lord shall renew their strength. They shall mount up with wings like eagles; they shall run and not be weary; they shall walk and not faint. (Isaiah 40: 31, TLB)

LOVE LETTERS

She still has his love letters, Father.

Neatly settled into a shoe box,
Tucked at the back of her cupboard,
She stores his letters.

He wrote them while they were courting,
    more than half a century ago.
I've not read them—
They are not mine to read—
But she reads them;
I've seen her.
She selects one carefully,
    holds it like a tiny chick,
    opens the pages gently,
    and reads quietly.
When she turns to greet me,
Her eyes are brimming.

Oh the power that words of love hold;
Words that endure
Through time and change.
The context is different,
But the sentiment, the message,
Unchanged.

Thank you for your love letters, Father.
I hold the Bible,
And read your words of love to me—
    to us—
Words that endure
Through time and change.
The context is different,
But the sentiment, the message,
Unchanged.

Heaven and earth will pass away, but my words will never pass away. (Matthew 24: 35, NIV)

JEWELLERY

She loves to wear her jewellery, Father.

It's not vanity,
Nor a display of affluence.
She wears them because they were gifts
From him—
    the man she gave her heart to so many decades
    ago;
    the man with whom she made a life;
    the man with whom she raised a family;
    the man who was by her side
        until he passed away.

So she wears the jewellery.
It's a symbol of his love.
It helps her to remember him
    and their life together.

It reminds me of the symbols of you, Father.
The cross,
    sign of the sacrifice made
    so that I could connect with you.
The Easter egg,
    sign of the empty tomb
    and new life I can find in you.
The candle,
    sign of your light,
    shining in a dark world.

Water,
>   sign of your cleansing
>   and satisfying our deepest thirst.

Bread,
>   sign of your body broken for us
>   and your life-giving nourishment.

Thank you for symbols
That help me to remember your love.

And he took bread, gave thanks and broke it, and gave it to them, saying, 'This is my body given for you; do this in remembrance of me.' In the same way, after the supper he took the cup, saying, 'This cup is the new covenant in my blood, which is poured out for you.' (Luke 22: 19–20, NIV)

AGEING

They're ageing, Father.

I look at my parents
And see their years piling on top of one another
    in their faces,
    in their posture,
    in their movement.

I've seen the family photos:
Images of young people
    marrying,
    smiling,
    holding infants,
    embracing children
        at picnics,
        parties,
        family celebrations.

The light is still in their eyes.
The love is still in their expressions.
The mischief still tickles their smile.

And Father, like their love for me,
Their love for you continues—
    perhaps grows—
Because of their experiences,
    their insights,
    their years.

Phil Ridden   *Reflections on faith inspired by seniors*

Life's trials have not dulled their faith,
> but polished it—
And it still shines.

Lead them into the future, Father.
Lead them into times and places
> where they may tell your story,
> where they may show your grace,
> where they may bring your love.

I'm ageing too, Father.
Is my faith still shining?
Is it being polished by my experiences of life
> and of you?

Youth may be admired for vigour, but grey hair gives prestige to old age. (Proverbs 20: 29, MSG)

DECAY

Her body is decaying, Father.

I see it each time I visit—
The body is weakening;
The hearing is fading;
The vision is blurring;
The speech is slurring;
The focus is going;
The responses are slowing.

But she knows I am here,
She knows I care.
Help me to renew her spirit for another day.

Help her to know you are here, too, Father.
Help her to know you care.
Renew her spirit day after day.

Even though our physical being is gradually decaying, yet our spiritual being is renewed day after day. And this small and temporary trouble we suffer will bring us a tremendous and eternal glory, much greater than the trouble. For we fix our attention, not on things that are seen, but on things that are unseen. What can be seen lasts only for a time, but what cannot be seen lasts forever. (Corinthians 4: 16–18, GNT)

ZIP

He had left his trouser zip undone, Father.

In his dressing, he had missed a step,
And now, amid a crowd,
His zip was so obviously undone.

I quietly whispered in his ear,
And he made the adjustment,
Laughing.

I think I often leave things undone, Father.
Not in my apparel,
But in my life,
In my service for you.
I like to think I have done what I ought,
Yet I know that there are things I've not done.
Show me what I've left undone, Father.

But woe to you Pharisees! For though you are careful to tithe even the smallest part of your income, you completely forget about justice and the love of God. You should tithe, yes, but you should not leave these other things undone. (Luke 11: 42, TLB)

THE FACE

That face, Father, has lived.

Like an oil painting on canvas,
The brush strokes,
And the patina,
Record life:
    love and happiness,
    despair and pain,
    pleasure and excitement,
    trauma and struggle—
All creased and worn and eroded
    into an image of joy and contentment.

Will my face be like that, Father?
Great paintings sometimes conceal earlier works,
    painted over;
The failed earlier attempt concealed
    beneath the exemplary work of the master.
I want my face
    to conceal my pain beneath my brushes with joy;
    to conceal my frustration beneath colours of contentment;
    to conceal my anguish beneath splashes of delight;
    to conceal my uncertainty beneath shades of certainty.

But we Christians have no veil over our faces; we can be mirrors that brightly reflect the glory of the Lord. And as the Spirit of the Lord works within us, we become more and more like him. (2 Corinthians 3: 18, TLB)

CUTTING UP FOOD

I had to cut up his food, Father.

Though an adult,
He is now unable to chew lumps of food,
And unable to cut them up himself,
So I do it for him.

We've come full circle,
For he once did this for me—
Cut up my food,
Because I was unable to chew lumps of food,
And unable to cut them up for myself.

My faith is a bit like that, Father.
Sometimes I struggle to cope,
To handle what life places before me,
And needing help to cut it into small pieces,
Of manageable size.

I know I ought to understand.
I know I ought to trust.
I know I ought to draw on my experience of you.
I know I ought to be able to help others.
But then, I revert to my immaturity—
    questioning when I ought to understand,
    complaining when I ought to trust,
    challenging when I ought to accept.

Phil Ridden   *Reflections on faith inspired by seniors*

Help me to grow, Father.
Feed me,
Piece by piece.

By this time you ought to be teachers yourselves, yet here I find you need someone to sit down with you and go over the basics on God again, starting from square one—baby's milk, when you should have been on solid food long ago! Milk is for beginners, inexperienced in God's ways; solid food is for the mature, who have some practice in telling right from wrong. (Hebrews 5: 11–14, MSG)

INSIGHT

They have learnt from life, Father.

When I was growing up,
And they were setting limits and rules,
I thought they were ignorant—
    of my needs,
    of the contemporary world,
    of teenagers,
    of pretty much anything that affected my life.
I saw the world through my lens only.

But deep down I knew—
And more and more I know—
That through their experiences,
They had acquired insight.
Deep down I wonder
    if I will ever be as wise as they.

They taught me so much
Through their gentle example
    and our conversations.
Best of all they taught me that
'The fear of the Lord is the beginning of wisdom.'

Thank you for parents who taught me to seek you.
Thank you for parents who serve you.
Thank you for parents who share what they have learnt.

Phil Ridden   *Reflections on faith inspired by seniors*

The way to become wise is to honour the Lord; he gives sound judgment to all who obey his commands. He is to be praised forever. (Psalm 111: 10, GNT)

LIKE HIM

'You're so like your Dad,' she said, Father.

Like him?
No.
I'm not like him.

He is aged.
A frame helps him walk;
The body is withered;
The face is ... well, old.
I'm not like him.

His narrow waist and broad mind have morphed
To broad waist and narrow mind.
I'm not like him.

His gentle patience is punctuated with irritability
Over simple things.
I'm not like him.

And yet, I am.
I don't want to admit it,
But I am—
    his values,
    his passion,
    his interests,

his faith,
　　his way of speaking,
　　his expressions ….
They pervade my life too.
I hear myself saying things he says;
Thinking things he thinks;
Becoming passionate about the things which ignite him.

Am I like this with you, Father?
Do I deny that I am made in your likeness,
That I have grown more and more like you?

She said, 'You're so like your Dad.'
Help me to live so that she also says,
'You are so like your eternal Father'—
Like you.

You imitated us and the Lord; and even though you suffered much, you received the message with the joy that comes from the Holy Spirit. So you became an example to all believers in Macedonia and Achaia. For not only did the message about the Lord go out from you throughout Macedonia and Achaia, but the news about your faith in God has gone everywhere. (1 Thessalonians 1: 6–8, GNT)

GIVING UP

I've seen old folk give up, Father.

They are unwell.
The body creaks and groans.
Their mind wanders.
They are lonely.
And they give up.
Some become impossible to please.
Some become gossips and trouble-stirrers.
Some retreat into isolation.
Some seek solace in alcohol.

But there are others—
Some who greet everyone with a smile.
Some who visit others to bring them cheer.
Some who read or talk or watch television with the lonely.
Some who walk every day, and encourage others to join them.
Some who bring your love,
    your good news,
    your compassion,
To everyone.

I want to be like that, Father—
Bringing your love to the world—

Always,
No matter how I age,
Always.

Guide older men into lives of temperance, dignity, and wisdom, into healthy faith, love, and endurance. Guide older women into lives of reverence so they end up as neither gossips nor drunks, but models of goodness. ... But mostly, show them all this by doing it yourself, incorruptible in your teaching, your words solid and sane. (Titus 2: 2–3, 8, MSG)

GREAT GRANDPARENTS

I took my children to see their great grandparents,
Father.

For the old folk it was a treat:
They love to see the kids,
To observe how they have grown,
To hear their stories of
    new adventures,
    new discoveries,
    new insights.

For the kids it was a treat:
They love to see Nanna and Poppa,
To hear their stories of the past,
To enjoy uninhibited affection,
    unreserved acceptance,
    unlimited food,
    unhurried time.

For me it was a treat:
I love to see them together—
These folk who helped to shape my life,
    helped to shape my faith,
    but are now in their final years;
And these little ones who now shape my life,
    and whose life I shape,
    while still in their early years.

Phil Ridden   *Reflections on faith inspired by seniors*

You loved me when I was beginning life, Father;
You loved me as I grew;
You continue to love me;
And you will love me to the end.

I will continue to love you,
    and to serve you,
        until my life's end.

The righteous will flourish like palm trees; they will grow like the cedars of Lebanon. They are like trees planted in the house of the Lord, that flourish in the Temple of our God, that still bear fruit in old age and are always green and strong. (Psalm 92: 12–14, GNT)

ALIKE

Am I really so much like them, Father?

I'm adopted.
So there's no 'geneticopying'.
Yet people say how alike we are.

Perhaps the reason we look like our parents
Is because we learn
    their expressions, their mannerisms.
It's there in
    the way we hold our head,
    the way we walk,
    the way we smile,
    the way we frown,
    our expressions when we concentrate
        or talk
        or laugh ...

I'm your child, Father.
Am I like you?

See what great love the Father has lavished on us, that we should be called children of God! And that is what we are! (1 John 3: 1, NIV)

DRIFTING

She's drifting, Father.

One moment, she is attentive:
    listening,
    comprehending,
    responding,
    even joking;
And then …
She is gone,
Drifting somewhere beyond my reach,
Unaware
    of my voice,
    my touch,
    even my presence.

Am I like that with you, Father?
Do I sometimes drift away,
Unaware
    of your voice,
    or your presence?

Your thoughts—how rare, how beautiful! God, I'll never comprehend them! I couldn't even begin to count them— any more than I could count the sand of the sea. Oh, let me rise in the morning and live always with you! (Psalm 139: 17–18, MSG)

GONE

She's gone, Father.

She was so much a part of our lives,
And now she is gone.

We know that death is a stage of life,
That it comes to us all,
And she had reached a fine age.
We know it,
We understand it,
We expected it.

But now she's gone,
To rest in your care for eternity;
And we who knew her and loved her,
We remain,
And we feel the reality
Of grief and loss.

Grant us comfort
With those who understand;
The comforting presence of
Your arm around our shoulders.

We give thanks for her love,
    for her friendship,
    for her example—
    for her life.

Phil Ridden   *Reflections on faith inspired by seniors*

Hers was a life to celebrate.
So bring joy to our mourning.
Help us to delight in the memories,
To laugh, and cry, and wonder
At a life well-lived,
And well loved.

Grant us your peace and joy.

Let your constant love comfort me, as you have promised me, your servant. (Psalm 119: 76, GNT)

By the same author:

Reflections on faith inspired by children
Reflections on faith inspired by seniors
Reflections on faith inspired by men
Reflections on faith inspired by babies
Reflections on faith inspired by COVID
Faith around the barbecue (The story)
Faith around the barbecue (The play)

Go to **www.philridden.biz**

www.ingramcontent.com/pod-product-compliance
Lightning Source LLC
Chambersburg PA
CBHW070433010526
44118CB00014B/2032